A Bike

by Violet Underwood
illustrated by Sigrid Darre

Practice Pre-Decodable 11

McGraw Hill Education

Bothell, WA • Chicago, IL • Columbus, OH • New York, NY

MHEonline.com

Send all inquiries to:
McGraw-Hill Education
8787 Orion Place
Columbus, OH 43240

ISBN: 978-0-02-141255-6
MHID: 0-02-141255-3

Printed in China.

9 10 11 12 13 DSS 27 26 25 24 23

The  has a  .

boy gift

The  has a  .

boy bike

The  has 4 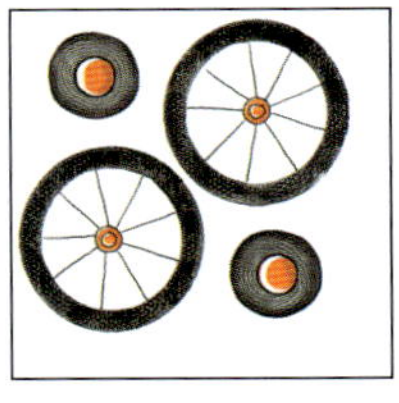.

bike four wheels

The  has .

boy Mom

The  has .

boy Dad

The  has 2 .

bike two wheels